*Without Warning*

For Virginia & Robert
Many thanks for
the support and
encouragement
and for bringing
me home.
 *[signature]*
3-18-'97

For Virginia & Robert -
Many thanks for
the Shepard art
and welcome
to the Lybring's
live library.
E.H.
3-18-97

49 Poems

ELIZABETH GOLDRING

B k M k PRESS  &  HELICON NINE EDITIONS
THE UNIVERSITY OF MISSOURI-KANSAS CITY    KANSAS CITY, MISSOURI

Copyright © 1995 by Elizabeth Goldring

All rights reserved under International and Pan-American Copyright Conventions.
Published by BkMk Press of the University of Missouri-Kansas City and
Helicon Nine Editions, Midwest Center for the Literary Arts, Inc.,
P. O. Box 22412, Kansas City, MO 64113

Earlier versions of some of these poems have been presented in the
following journals, catalogues, public exhibitions, and conferences:
*Asylum* Annual, 1994; *Center Poems, 1991*; Charlotte Moorman Memorial,
Whitney Museum of American Art, February 15, 1991;
*LightsOROT*, Yeshiva University Museum Catalogue, 1987;
The New England Journal of Optometry, March 1990;
The Sky Art Conference '81, MIT, Cambridge, MA, 1981; and
UNESCO conference and publication, "Babel," Cologne, 1992
Eye/Sight poetry (audiotape) installations at:
Yeshiva University Museum, 1987; Kunstverein, Karlsruhe, 1988;
Savonlinna, Finland, 1989; Washington Project for the Arts,
Washington, D.C., 1991; and MIT Museum, Cambridge, MA, 1994.

Cover image: Otto Piene, *Scarlet*, tempera on paper, 1995
Book design: Tim Barnhart

Partial funding for this book was provided by
the National Endowment for the Arts, a federal agency;
the Missouri Arts Council and the Kansas Arts Commission, state agencies;
and the N.W. Dible Foundation.

Library of Congress Cataloging-in-publication Data

Goldring, Elizabeth.
   Without warning : 49 poems / Elizabeth Goldring. - - 1st ed.
     p.   cm.
    ISBN 1-884235-13-1  (alk. paper)
    I. Title.
PS3557.O3846W58    1995
811'.54 - - dc20                                                             95-8899
                                                                                        CIP

FIRST EDITION
Printed in the United States of America.

For my parents,
Otto,
Jessica,
Bär (1984-1994),
and Elizabeth Hua

# Contents

- 9   Motorola Morning
- 10   Aztec Moon
- 11   Lone Pine, CA
- 13   Killer Machine
- 14   On the Boston and Maine Train
- 15   A Child Balances the Weight of a Ruler on Two Index Fingers
- 17   Beaches
- 18   Valentine
- 19   Roosters Don't Fly
- 21   Tall Buildings
- 22   Kyoto
- 23   Goulimine
- 24   The Way to M'Namid
- 25   Taroudant, Morocco
- 26   Todos Santos
- 27   At a Gas Pump Near Gordes
- 28   Souvenir (November 11, 1989)
- 29   Leipzig Journal (November 6-11, 1989)
- 31   Leukemia
- 32   Stan
- 33   Restraint
- 34   For Charlotte
- 35   Paper Cello
- 37   Sometimes He Just Wanted to Sit with a Beer and Watch the Game
- 39   Blue Haven (Tobago, 1987)

| | |
|---|---|
| 40 | Speaking Tongues |
| 41 | Pittsburgh Secrets |
| 42 | Afterglow |
| 43 | Socks |
| 44 | Advent |
| 45 | One Late Afternoon A Week After My Daughter Started Middle School in Cambridge, MA |
| 46 | Four Days After You Left |
| 47 | The Ashford Motel |
| 48 | Driving Away from Pine Ridge Your Profile Drenched in Rain |
| 49 | Grandma's Garden |
| 50 | Farm Stories |
| 51 | Gedächtniskirche |
| 52 | Sunflowers |
| 53 | Yoyo |
| 54 | Orange Monarchs |
| 55 | Anesthesia Amnesia |
| 56 | Post Op |
| 57 | Morning Glory |
| 58 | Stained Glass |
| 59 | Sole Survivor |
| 60 | Don't Break My Amulet |
| 61 | The Electronics of Blindness |
| 62 | She Construction |
| 63 | I Need a Metaphor |
| | |
| 64 | About the Author |

## MOTOROLA MORNING

My heart's a beamed up Motorola morning.
Cradling my head in the crook of his arm
his thighs twitching ever so slightly
we watch TV.
Nothing happens
except politics,
murder in Roxbury,
arson in Lynn
and
early morning fog
in low lying areas
with treacherous patches of ice
on secondary arteries and roadways.

Nothing happens
except
the blurring nausea of a colliding room.
He gets up to walk the dogs.
Full sails grown
like chinese paper flowers
collapse in the suction of his leaving.

## AZTEC MOON

Electronic bees
surge.
I cower,
razored by information
grazing my temples.

Fly over Teotichuacan today.
You'll see it all—
knees inching up to the altar,
Jerusalem roosters,
yellow fever,
German measles,
med fly,
Montezuma.

Time's running out.
Hands fall off the clock.
Stop
the Age of Aquarius.
Stop
calling hate
disease.

## LONE PINE, CA

A big foot leaps to a mile,
a giant's thumbnail,
a penis bigger than Caesar.

Long arms and dough feet
reach up from very old hearts
once fired in clay furnaces.
All the hard geometry is bucked
by quiet.
Pulsebeats
never stop throbbing
inside those doughboy legs.

Out there
clean jaws and snow white teeth
bite the sky;
here—
kissing mouths,
ears rumbling with bees,
giant pagodas in the thought of erection.

Indigo flowers
darker than sun
bloom deep
in familiar crevasses
pungent with odors.

There's life in these stone breasts,
armpits and old asses
lathed over centuries of wind and hate.
Ancient thighs cough the breath of coyote,
raven and rattlesnake.

The buzz,

the golden circle
cool first.

Love making
wet with years of growing old,
megalithic hugs,
tortured whispers,
crushed sage,
anneal boulder hearts,
black rose lips and swaying towers
painted in ochres,

a hundred miles off
DEATH VALLEY.

## KILLER MACHINE

smiles run from your eyes and mouth corners
sound of smiles
hear them
run on
like a nickelodeon

smiles run from your eyes and mouth corners
not too heavy chains
twang
electric shocks
breaths of concentration

smiles
fresh glass
rain
not too heavy chains
twang electric shock
waves
not
breaths of concentration

Play it
jaws spread

sickle smile
sits there
like a pretty object
clasps
skins too rough to touch
must be cut up
for sharks,
dolphins

It's just
legs for now

## ON THE BOSTON AND MAINE TRAIN
(In and Out of Waltham Station)

    1. IN

The train stops
short of a drunk
leapin' over the tracks.
He claims the train's hit him.
There's a big stink.
The train's delayed.
The drunk ambles on board
arm in a sling
smellin' pretty.
He squeezes a plump leg with his free hand.

    2. OUT

A black lady screams
fuck.
She scorns her sisters
for wearin' green contacts;
lookin' like cats.
She informs them all
she shaved the fur off her yellow lab
to find out if he was white or black.
Whatdoya know, she says,
There's no black dogs.

# A CHILD BALANCES THE WEIGHT OF A RULER ON TWO INDEX FINGERS

RULER
    one:  he who rules
          a sovereign king
          (Webster's Seventh Edition)
And who is she?
    two:  a worker or a machine that rules
          (e.g. paper)
    three:  a smooth edged strip used for guiding
          (e.g. a pencil or pen)

RULER:  REULE
         REGULA
         REGERE

To lead straight

the king's foot
the aura
the crown
the measuring stick

measured
measurable
measurably
(e.g. contended, questioned, dreamed)

cogs, wheels,
tracks through the cosmos

sea
branch
tree

All dead kings and kings to be
living forms and bronze cast tragedy
the green inchworm
scurrying across the marble index
of Caesar's colossal finger

It's a measure
even when she saws it off.

# BEACHES

The man with a wave for his tongue
licks the beach
Pyramids burn in his eyes
His saber winnows her shores
His hoofs poun   d      her
pe   bbl   es into  in  d i vis  i   b  le
ingots of stars

*on she dreams*
*sleeping with horses*

# VALENTINE

The field of snow ate new snow
until its cheeks blew out whiter than the snow it ate.
Clacking bird silhouettes break over
a blond woman wearing a red coat—
iridescent red.
She falls belly up,
dragging her wide coat sleeves through the snow
so that her trench becomes a valentine.
She ponders the sequence in French:
 *champs de neige, mangeant la neige,*
 *les choux, les ailes des oiseaux,*
 *le manteau rouge,*
 *le trencher,*
 *les manches mouvementées, vues par les oiseaux,*
 *les massacres au jour Saint Valentin qui rougit*
 *la neige.*

## ROOSTERS DON'T FLY

> *Japanese rooster masters hold annual contests for the rooster with the longest tail and the rooster with the longest crow.*

Tangled Lorelei
perched in trees
comb tails assessed at thirteen meters

Big blue sky
bitten by winged victories
Star surveyors mark high nests,
black holes,
fifty thousand layers

Tibetan hermits ooze cannon fire,
malaria,
heroes,
magic,
the blackened red of kites

Dying wasps
join oligarchies of white dwarves
hatching in vats of unblown glass

Open highway
get up and go
leave—take off
"No need for wings," rooster said
Ba and Ka and angel fled

Roosters
crow long
and loud
Best time's clocked at thirteen seconds

One day I followed the longest tail
to the tip of the tallest cockscomb
—Dodge City—
low sky
high mirage
rage
hommage
loft
aloft

We are climbing higher, higher
Cormorant dives
Eagle
rises
purple

Rocket
feathers
fall

yellow flame
yellow star
yellow sky

black flame
black star
black sky

Rooster flame
Rooster star
Rooster sky

## TALL BUILDINGS

Tall buildings
zip down their flies
zip up their flies

Tall buildings
leap in glass elevators
going up

Tall buildings
stuck on twelve
going down

KYOTO
tea
                    CAMBRIDGE
ceremony            MA

1. There must be no sound
of water
in the Japanese garden
2. No sound of water
3. No smell of flower
and yet
4. The full moon shone
5. through the open door
onto a porch of phosphorescing angels
—wing flapping seraphims
—laughing dolls
despite the artifice of a Cambridge backyard
and two U.S. fags
6. dressed in kimono
7. serving tea

# GOULIMINE

Black hands finger
red castles

Night tracks
white across the sky

Wise old camel
dowses
yellow bricks

Blue Sahara man beckons.

    Black dust

    Yellow road

It hasn't rained for nine years.

# THE WAY TO M'NAMID
(where the real Sahara begins)

Mud lives in mud houses
mud goats and donkeys.
Mud cakes on the runway to the sun.
Red-earth fathers
Rulers of adobe
The palm oasis wraps its moustache hairs
around each fallen Kasbah.
New fingers layer taller, grander towers
over the Draa.

The river stops at the last town
where widows dart like chicks in sand,
and tanks loom
sudden as the desert.

# TAROUDANT, MOROCCO

*YOU ARE WELCOME.*
*I AM AT YOUR SERVICE.*
Layered petals wrap
the ladies.
Their daughters are
not shy.
*Dallas* on TV
has set them free.
Their eyes are shining
with tables of fruit.

What happened
last night
between four and six
before the *muezzin*
calls again?
The lingering madness
of an unplayed note
fires up her heart.

The blue veil
falls from her face.
Her bare hand with a
white palm
ever so white
waves,
and she says
from a mouth purple
with life

*BONJOUR!*

## TODOS SANTOS

Woman gathers the family
builds the fire
collects the ashes
lays the picnic
folds the napkins

When the urn is lowered
she spits into the fresh dirt
dons her black habits
stirs tepid coffees
rolls out next year's
candy   pink   skeletons

## AT A GAS PUMP NEAR GORDES

Plump white hat
pushed back,
she sniffs the turgid marshes,
figs and fruits of the valley,
purple wines and home-grown cheeses.
Winds scenting her nostrils,
she leans back,
soaks it all in.
Her stomach bulging,
she pumps benzine
at her filling station off N 100.

# SOUVENIR
(November 11, 1989)

The Wall is a zone
Nothing moves
Protection
The Wall is Jericho
The Wall is lighted
by the full moon that floats across it
The shadow of a shadow
The Wall is stopped velocity
Too high to piss over

The Wall is a set of watch towers
The Wall is architecture
An accretion
An erection
Landfill

The Wall is a Trojan Horse
The Wall is the difference between Mercedes-Benz
and perestroika
The Wall is open to the sky
Perpendicular
A parameter
A lesson

The Wall is a rosary of lies
The Wall is the hem on a skirt of inequities
The Wall is an outcry
The Wall is a pastiche
A political asterisk

A souvenir
Sold piecemeal

# LEIPZIG JOURNAL
(November 6-11, 1989)

Pale leaves paper the cobbles.
Loose steam rises up from somewhere
underneath,
vague as the gallery of nudes
downtown.

Wives peer into empty shops,
wishing they had something to buy for Christmas.
There are no dogs to curb.
At four p.m. the shadow of Bach falls on his church.

Monday, after prayers,
the wide compass of ring-linked boulevards
swells to 300,000.

The city government resigns.
There's no other party,
no roving cats,
no homeless people.
Helmet eyes watch from steeples.
The mass is greater than the height.

Friday, The Wall cracked:
the city levitated like a hot air balloon
burning old shoes for flame.

Eat bananas.
The real bash is in the West
where fat grins shine through busy teeth,
gold rims,
black Mercedes.

Stinking chariots cough across the border.

Behold the blaze of red and purple sunsets,
while herds of deer press East
fleeing ideology,
*Democracy,*
*democratic ideals.*

Western guys will rape your brides,
their cannibal hearts
full throttle.

## LEUKEMIA
*for Betsy Waldron,*
*who wanted to be an artist*

She pulled the darkest
most luminous fantasies seen anywhere
out of her cauldron,
dripping self-portraits,
smashed spokes of fences,
quadrants of night on holographic film.
She touched white heat:
her hair,
electric coils;
her eyes,
magnetic poles.
She dreamt of bogs,
vanished
crossing the street.

Cambridge
8 September, 1987
(at the intersection of
Vassar and Mass. Ave.)

# STAN

His bones
dangle from the necklace
of his first wife
He is ashes
He is pieces
He is alabaster skin
and yellow hair
He is flying high
He is magic
He is god

## RESTRAINT
(mourning the death of a poet)

He's there for me in the objects he tagged,
books he marked,
boxes of bells he left for me to hang in the wind.

On his death I got a check.
He speaks to me now in the language of money,
societies of trees,
nature relief funds,
causes I'm discovering
he believed in.

My song for him
tied to a bell
rings out entrails of storms,
seasons,
stopping my memory of poems.

# FOR CHARLOTTE
(censored hero of The Opera Sextronique*)
# DYING HERO IN YOUR FIGHT WITH CANCER

You played your cello wired, topless,
under water,
coming out of Kosugi's blue bag.
You made ice cellos, chocolate cellos, human cellos,
bombs, T.V.s.
You played cello fish, cellos at Guadalcanal,
red crosses pinned to Josef Beuys' felts.

When Otto Piene said he'd fly you from his helium flower,
you didn't believe your luck.
You, fastened to a grand bouquet of helium-filled,
polyethylene loops, 200 foot-long tubes bent in half.
You, a cello strumming, flying sculpture, a sky angel,
floating out across the Danube, "somewhere in Austria,"
going up to 300 feet,
maybe higher.

For the premiere of "Sky Kiss"
you wore your custom-padded parachute harness,
your green gown and white satin cape.
Otto checked the ropes himself.
He didn't want to lose you,
wouldn't let you disappear
like a Queen.

Groton
November, 1991

---
*by Nam June Paik

# PAPER CELLO
*following an earlier version read February 15, 1992
at the Charlotte Moorman Memorial,
Whitney Museum of American Art, New York*

A bald shopkeeper
in Karlsruhe
inched up the ladder.
Far out of reach,
behind the faded rainbows,
he found an angel
stringing the cello.

You said you liked it
and you set it out
with your what-nots.

You said you liked it and you set it out on the lighted, glassed-in what-not shelves that Frank built to house your collection of dolls—your passion for hearts and Arkansas diamonds, and all the kitsch you killed for up and down the boardwalk in Atlantic City. You loved to save and fondle these treasures, the way folks do.

You always remembered my birthday, the day before Valentine's Day, your favorite holiday. I've kept the presents you sent:

1 brass heart
1 cut glass heart
1 plastic heart filled with medium-size shells
1 marble heart tied with pink ribbons and filled with miniature shells
a pair of George and Barbara Bush slippers
1 porcelain heart frame
1 frosted heart candle
a cherry-scented candle decorated with cupids

a penis-shaped heart vase filled with 11 chiffon roses
The paper shadow of your cello, embedded with shamrocks, that you
made in Italy, one year before you died

That night
I was crying with Frank on the phone.
You passed through in a swirl of gold and purple lingerie.
Frank said
your last words were,
"I want a banana."

# SOMETIMES HE JUST WANTED TO SIT WITH A BEER AND WATCH THE GAME

One and a half years since Charlotte died
Frank's getting ready.
At first he was relieved
not to have to give her morphine
nine times a day,
not to have to watch Charlotte dying.
Then he began to find her notes
hidden among the heaps of stuff in their loft—
things even he could not have known,
although he never left except to run for
morphine.

When I called Frank on Monday, late,
he didn't tell me he would die.
He did say, if the auction went wrong
he'd jump off the roof.
It wasn't a joke the way he said it,
but he promised to call on Friday.

At Sotheby's in London
half of Charlotte's estate sold.
Not bad for bad times.
Frank's heart began to tear,
an aneurysm in his aorta.
The day after the auction it burst.

We said goodbye to Frank
and to our views on saints
at the open casket in Brooklyn—
to the body, not Frank's face,
not his eyes,
not his hands or shoulders.

Frank, long gone of course,
we said to be with Charlotte.

I hear his voice razz the wire
warm, reassuring.
His voice still hangs around,
promising to call.

## BLUE HAVEN
(Tobago, 1987)

You never leave me
except to draw a face
or watch a diving pelican.
It doesn't matter
how little I see.
Our steps curl with the waves
and flapping trees.

One cruise ship passes
close to shore.
One pod drops.
One hibiscus wilts.
One palm leaf
splits.

The Blue Haven,
closed,
abandoned,
sold.

We won't go there anymore.

## SPEAKING TONGUES

Voices put mouths
around sound
Mouth
sounds
Suck in
spaces
behind tongues
Shape
mouths to
voices

I grab his shiny tie and pull
For the first time I see him in a line
from chin to forehead
For the first time he looks surprised

## PITTSBURGH SECRETS

*I asked if you were the artist*
*who floated the Red Skyline over Pittsburgh*
*and lifted a ninety-two pound girl*
*into Equilibrium.*

It was my first time in Pittsburgh,
I weighed a hundred and twenty-four pounds.
It's an expensive lift, you said.

We rode the light funicular,
bridging rivers,
sponging skies.
Waitresses gliding like cymbals
pinned tails on donkeys.

Back at the hotel,
cigars skunked the elevator.
It's an expensive lift, you said.

I was your birthday—
*sixteen years ago,*
*in Pittsburgh.*

## AFTERGLOW
(postcoital sparks)

Egg
breaks
over
hen coals.
Raw white
eyes
shine through
baby pink.
Starched
tits
poke through
veils of fire.
Your face
dances
like the Basque ritual
(Burgos heads
wreathed in leaves
lighted on fire)
burning
to ox-blood
embers.

# SOCKS

Walking the tread mill
I watch the socks get in front of each other.
I'm mesmerized by their red color
and the idea that they're your socks.
I've worn them without asking you.
Even if you won't walk the tread mill
your socks have gotten mixed up with my feet.
They're our socks.
I grin despite the friction of tread mill
and walking feet.

# ADVENT

I see your smoke in the clouds.
I feel you coming.
You land,
Swiss Air, as usual.

I am Yule,
wearing my hat
at the airport,
as usual.
You do not see me,
walk right by me
up to the change counter
out the doors
onto the curb
into a taxi.

## ONE LATE AFTERNOON
## A WEEK AFTER MY DAUGHTER STARTED
## MIDDLE SCHOOL IN CAMBRIDGE, MA

A little cat, a little dog, a little girl in a Joseph's hat and blue coat walk with me. She looks pink in a world of animal and forest. We pass a school of Christmas trees, two footers, some pale green and fading, others dark, plump. Beyond the field a trail breaks into woods. Deep trees hang like mushrooms against the waning day.

On our way back, Queen Anne's Lace ball into *fleurs du mal* among the landing crows.

## FOUR DAYS AFTER YOU LEFT

I thought I felt the bedsheets move
of course not
I thought I heard a pillow shift
of course not
I thought I touched a piece of thigh
I thought I caught your whiff of breath
I thought you spoke
No, I'm mistaken
The phone's dead
No
hello

# THE ASHFORD MOTEL

I wish your eyes
could still see mine
I wish you could
tell me what you feel
not what you know

I wish we would drive to Ashford

I wish this were
a phase
that you would
ask me questions

I wish
you didn't hate routine
I wish
I didn't hate routine
I wish
the plants would die

I can see
without seeing
I can hear
without hearing
I can come
without coming
but not the leaving

## DRIVING AWAY FROM PINE RIDGE
## YOUR PROFILE DRENCHED IN RAIN

Two straws drink hot
Injun Joe
Machine vibrations
make me blink
Headlights drown:

Eyes flood
Can't speak
Can't see to know
Can't hear what
Say I love you

## GRANDMA'S GARDEN (1915-1993)
Bradgate, Iowa

I was there as a child
strawberries,
bachelor buttons,
garden pinks, behind them
the glads
They stretched from the house to the outhouse,
next to Mrs. Pugsly's garden

Last summer crossing Iowa
I spotted Bradgate in the Mississippi,
angled up and sinking fast,
oozing life's last air
Flooded flowers,
soaked to the gills

I heard her garden drown

# FARM STORIES

1) October Fire

The red leaves won't lie down;
they tap at the windows,
flirt to get in.
Anger gleams in their nipples.
Cool stones rinse their eyes.
They are not shaved,
grin to come in,
beg to lie down
everywhere.


2) Clean Winter

I'm waiting for the silver fox.
Soon his blue voice will cloud the moonlight
and his breath will catch against the snow.


3) Spring Floods

Rain's pounding inside my head.
New rivers flow from my eye-holes and nostrils.
Turtles fork seawings out of the mud.
Their wet tweets announce
another quicksand savior.


4) The Farm Wife

Her lantern draws water.
He is far away,
far as green glitter.

Asparagus
stands loose in the field.

GEDÄCHTNISKIRCHE
(Memorial Church in Berlin,
Rebuilt in the '50s)

I crave the blue
It chews me
Its teeth eat my heart out

Blue bones
Blue fire
Anger is blue
Blue chants
melt in blue coffee

Blue without breath
Blue without fire
Blue stamens bring a red poppy

## SUNFLOWERS

They smash
headlong
onto green earth
Yellow bonnets tangle
Faces bulge

(Molly Bloom
caught ripe
too heavy
too full
too soon
falls off her stem)

Upturned here and there
vague, sunny stares
go slack

Dark glasses
from then on

# YOYO

I don't believe in the prairie twister
slamming onto the frozen ground.
I don't believe in seasons of croaking frogs
and dying moths.

I don't believe in omens,
witches,
the car crash that leaves one kid in a coma,
kills the other.

I'm falling
with nauseating speed.
Things miss;
have happened;
have not happened,
yet.

Will I toss and turn
under the paws of the she wolf,
forever?

I want to see a star
bloom from the heart of an oak.
I want to split palm fronds
and blow sirocco,
anytime.

I want my eyes back.

## ORANGE MONARCHS
an ether dream

Black gas
leeches
make a
blood sucking
diving suit
of my skin.
Their lamps
shine.

Caterpillars
crawl inside
my nose
escaping
the leeches.

Rubber nose holes
hatch orange wings,
bug off to South America.
It's Butterfly Candyland.

# ANESTHESIA AMNESIA

This hearth reflects nothing,
no glimmer of crystal
or traces of coal.
*Bocca della verita*—
once, I saw it
standing in the corner of a Roman church—
quiet as a locomotive under glass,
still as the bloodless death of a child.

This hole knows no bat,
no squirrel,
no locust.
It stares back at me
like the muzzle of my breathing mask.
The last thing I remembered:

*a double pink hibiscus.*

# POST OP

Micro-surgeons have drained my eyes.
I look in the mirror
at the glasses on my face.
I don't see my face
but images outside the window
pour into the mirror
through my lenses:

> Dog jumping
> Sun on wheat
> Blue
> Van Gogh
> Sun
> Green
> White flash
> Black
> Bird
> Fly into light

Smiling string
Leaps into yellow pails
Crows red
Shoots black
Into
Yellow black
Revolver

# MORNING GLORY
### *(paraphrase for Paul Eluard)*

Two days after surgery
the doctor unwraps my eye.
Her pencil red lips
burst into Red Lips
without Warning.
The sky out the window
fills with assassins,
trampolines.
Flashes of sight
jump between answers and questions.
Pictures steer my mind.
Sparklers.
Reason's a cloud
parodied by the moon.

Her pencil red lips
burst
without Warning.

## STAINED GLASS

I sit in the crypt of starry Sainte Chapelle.
The stars dim. They don't blink.

a jagged flash
light
crashes through
the painted
night

unplugged rods and cones
purple traffic
green river phosphenes
sand beaches

I blink.
Lights stay in droves—
adenoids to blackness,
misfirings,
misguided currents.

My brain is popping bleeps.

## SOLE SURVIVOR

I'll wait until they're gone
and I'm blind,
only their poems
on my mind.

# DON'T BREAK MY AMULET
(for diabetics)

Holding my toe,
I sit next to eight pregnant women.
We wait to be seen.

Doctors carry plastic
calves and feet
in and out of closets.

Love, I want you
to be

Later, at the dentist
I'm being jellied for a bridge.
My teeth
shake.
Quiet, you pack of wolves.
My feet go
ape.

*Chief Rain-in-the-Bag,*
I love you

## THE ELECTRONICS OF BLINDNESS

Electric octave drops to blue tone.
My eyes are portable TVs.
My sight's a bloody vigil.
Magnetic fields grip bits of decomposing blood
like wasps sucking honey.

Eyes monitor isolation.
A man fastens his ladder to a truck.
Beyond the peptic green light
violet eagles rise,
tracked on both my eyes.

## SHE CONSTRUCTION

Everybody loses a watch,
trips,
faints,
gets depressed.
I kick the crocheted doorstop lady
(with token eyes)
flat on her back,
slam the door.
I'm the parenthesis
(earth and moon),
the Maenad go-between
where waves rock.
Lasers etch my soul fish pink.

Would I rather be someone else?
Maybe, once, (Elizabeth).

# I NEED A METAPHOR

My feet toughen
Toe ends yellow
I see what happens
Every word becomes a sign:
    Chairs stand for fortitude
    A table,
    horizontal boredom
    Travel,
    orgiastic pain
    Erasmus, maybe,
    the dead.
It's my toes that first expose memory—
    flooded skating rinks,
    frozen feet,
    hands stinging,
    skin on skin,
    tingling lips
    stuck to hot cider.
Our eyes stood still,
pressing sweet, incalculable cold
into souls we could not bare
enough to see.

## About the Author

Elizabeth Goldring's first book of poems is *Laser Treatment* (Blue Giant Press, Boston, 1983). She has presented her poetry, multi-media performances, and environments at exhibitions, events, and festivals in Europe and the United States. Together with Otto Piene she co-directed the International Sky Art Conferences from 1981-86.

Her videotapes include "The Inner Eye: From the Inside Out" (with Vin Grabill), "A Visual Language for the Blind" (with Robert Webb), and "Toward Interactive Television Environments for the Blind" (with Vin Grabill). She has co-edited *Centerbeam* (MIT Press, 1980); *Center Poems* (CAVS/MIT, 1991); The Sky Art Conference (CAVS/MIT, 1981).

Elizabeth Goldring is a Research Fellow and Exhibits and Projects Director at MIT's Center for Advanced Visual Studies (CAVS). She has also served as acting co-director of CAVS and has held an appointment in the Department of Architecture at MIT, where she has taught seminars in art and environmental poetry.

For the past ten years Goldring has been devoted to visualizing vision loss and creating the poetics of a visual language for people with low vision. In her experiments in "Retinal Poetry" she currently uses a Scanning Laser Ophthalmoscope (SLO). Her "eye journals" documenting her own vision loss and periods of blindness form an important basis for her poetry.

She and her husband, Otto Piene, live on a farm in Groton, Massachusetts, and in Düsseldorf.